Disturbed by God

Disturbed by God is offered
to the glory of God in thanksgiving
for the many blessings and learnings of life
which come in the "disturbances"

It is dedicated
to my son Tod Maffin
for his courage
in allowing his story to be shared
and for his continuing openness
to the Holy Spirit's activity in his life.

Thanks be to God.

"And a little child shall lead them"
Isaiah 11:6b

Disturbed by God

A Journey of Spiritual Discovery

June Maffin

Anglican Book Centre
Toronto, Canada

1996
Anglican Book Centre
600 Jarvis Street
Toronto, Ontario
M4Y 2J6

Canadian Cataloguing in Publication Data

Maffin, June Mack
    Disturbed by God : a journey of spiritual discovery

ISBN 1-55126-153-7

1. Maffin, June Mack.   2. Spiritual biography.
3. Spiritual life – Anglicans.   I. Title.

BV4011.6.M3 1996   248.4   C96-930164-2

Contents

Preface

Dear Reader,

We often overlook those moments when God speaks to us, the times when God "disturbs" our lives. Could it be that we miss those moments, because we tend to look for dramatic evidence of God's direction when ordinary instances abound, if only we were aware of them?

Although this book is a record of God's disturbances in my life, you may want to use it to reflect on your own faith journey and to become more aware of God's disturbances in your life.

Before beginning to read, you might find it helpful to refer to some of the sections at the back of the book, particularly the one on keeping a Prayer Journal. The book is in three main sections.

1. Framed by the poetry of the Prologue and Epilogue, the Chapters narrate the life story of an ordained woman.

2. The Reflection Starters, which follow each section of that narrative, include questions which (*through the use of a Prayer Journal or group discussion*) might

   * stimulate prayerful attention to the "*God-incidences*" in your life (those incidents you may have ignored or not noticed or forgotten),

- challenge deeper reflection about your *baptismal ministry,*
- enhance your understanding of Anglicanism.

3. The final sections of the book provide information to help you work with the material in the Chapters and the Reflection Starters. Along with short lists of recommended books for further reading, they include

  - Methods for Reflection (individual and group study),
  - Approaches to Prayer,
  - Glossary of Terms.

The Reflection Starters can be used by one or by many. If people wish to study as a group, they might work individually on one section of five chapters during the five weekdays, and then come together on the weekends to discuss their findings (please see Methods for Reflection, pp. 115 – 120). In this way, the six main sections of the book could provide a six-week course.

As you read through *Disturbed by God*, perhaps you'll experience some "ah-hah" moments (times when your spirit resonates with instances of God disturbing your life) and moments when you experience an invitation to a deeper relationship with the One who loves you unconditionally. I pray that this is so.

May your daily journey with the One who called you into being, continue to "disturb" your life in ways that are exciting, challenging, and fulfilling!

God bless!

June Maffin

Prologue

My life is content. Why disturb it?

Okay!
I'll come to church
and listen to the choir.

But really, those sermons seem to go on forever.
The people stare at me.
And I don't know where I am in the service book.

I feel
awkward
unwelcome
ignorant.

Besides,
who is this God
they all close their eyes for
and pray to?

My life is content. Why disturb it?

But —
something is happening.
There's something (*some One?*)
urging me
to learn about who God is!
Why?

Okay!
I'll attend Bible Study.
I won't sneak out the back door of the church
during sermon time.
I will try to follow and understand the service.

But I feel
uncertain
inadequate
ill-prepared.

Besides,
I'm not sure I want to know
much more
about this
God.

My life is content. Why disturb it?

The urge compels me further.
Ask questions.
(No rejections? Childhood memories: Cease!)
Ask more questions.
(But more questions arise — not answers.)

The urge compels me yet further . . .
Be baptized.
(Nothing happened. What did I expect?)

Ask people to pray for me.
(They did!)

Seek Confirmation.
(Why can't I feel terrific about this?)
Confirmed,
because I want to get closer to God.

What?
Is God that much a part of my life now?

Yes
Yes
Yes

Beginnings

In the beginning, God…
— Genesis 1:1

Chapter One

When did God begin to "disturb" my life? That's not an easy question.

I'm still in the process of unravelling all the God-incidences — those times when God invited me to journey into new and uncharted territories, disturbing my familiar and safe spiritual haven.

Having been raised in a non-mainline church, I knew at an early age that God loved me. But who was God? When I asked questions, I was given stock responses. "Accept what you're told. Don't question."

Don't question? If God created me — body, mind, and spirit — then why couldn't I use my mind to learn more? Why couldn't I ask questions? Not to use my mind was to say "No thanks" to God for the gift given. At the age of fifteen, I left the church which I felt denied me the encouragement to use God's gift of reason.

Many years later, I married the choir director of a local Anglican church. Because I thought it was the expected thing to do, I went with him to church each Sunday. But people seemed more interested in meeting their friends than greeting a newcomer in their midst. So, each Sunday, I sat at the back of the church, alone, trying to follow the service.

A friend of mine (not a churchgoer) invited me to have a

cup of tea with her on Sunday mornings. She lived just a few doors away from the church. After being visible in church until the choir had sung its anthem, I slipped out to visit with my friend. But I always made sure that I was back in time for coffee hour, so that I could greet my husband, give him feedback about the music, and socialize with other parishioners.

This went on for months. How my friend and I regaled ourselves with laughter! We thought of the "pious ones" sitting on hard wooden benches while we sat comfortably on her couch, sipping tea and nibbling raisin bread.

One Sunday, I returned before people had left the church. As I couldn't avoid the line-up to greet the priest, I stood in line, shook his hand, said something inane like, "Lovely service," and attempted to move on.

Then came God's first overt "disturbance" in my life.

The priest kept holding my hand and, with a gentle smile, said, "Thank you. Oh, by the way, we're having Bible Study classes this Thursday morning. You're welcome to join us."

Bible Study? Thanks, but no thanks! I didn't want some person telling me what to believe. I'd left a church years ago for that reason. Why would I want to repeat the incident? But rather than explaining, I returned his smile and said, "Thank you, but no."

Not taking No for an answer, he continued. "Well, if you're available, come Thursday morning. Just show up and try us out. No strings attached." Whatever did he mean by, "No strings attached"? Did he know I was leery of Bible Study? This was curious.

For an ever-so-brief moment, I wondered if this had something to do with God.

Wednesday came and, oddly, I remembered that the next day was Bible Study. I argued with myself, "I'm not going to get involved in a group which passively sits and listens to some apparent expert cram his personal opinions into us."

Thursday morning, promptly at 6:00 a.m., I woke up, completely rested. It seemed that all I could think of was Bible Study! What was happening? I couldn't explain it. In quick order, my son was fed and taken to preschool, my household chores were completed, and I found myself at the church in time for Bible Study.

Eventually I became a regular Bible Study participant. And this time, I discovered that it was all right to ask questions. It was all right to question the Bible and what I believed. It was all right to question the church's stand on certain issues. Through questioning came more questions, but through those questions came clarity, insight, and resolution.

God's disturbance was unsettling at first, but it was the beginning of a wonderfully exciting spiritual journey.

Reflection Starters One

Have you ever been at a service of worship, a Christian social gathering, workshop, conference, or so on — not knowing why you were there, yet sensing that it was "right" that you were there?

How did you respond? Note that response in your Prayer Journal.*

What questions do you have about

- the Bible?
- your faith?
- the church's stand on certain issues?

Note those questions at the back of your Prayer Journal. As you gain insights about the questions, note those insights in your Prayer Journal.

Has God ever used a clergyperson to "disturb" your life? Reflect on that situation in your Prayer Journal.

Have you ever been involved in Bible Study? Did God ever "disturb" your life in any of those Bible Study sessions? Describe that disturbance in your Prayer Journal.

How did you respond? Note that response in your Prayer Journal.

*You may want to refer to the entry on keeping a Prayer Journal in the Methods for Reflection section at the end of this book.

Chapter Two

I soon stopped my Sunday morning tea visits and began to pay attention to the Sunday worship — even cautiously moving forward a pew or two as the weeks passed.

Slowly, questions about the liturgy emerged.

My background in a non-liturgical religious tradition encouraged me to wonder about many things — the uniformity and formality of dress worn by presiders at the liturgy; the focus on a large table on a raised platform at the front of the church; the use of different coloured fabrics at different times of the year to cover the table; the practice of lighting one candle on that table before the other; the importance of involving the worshippers as participants, rather than observers, in the service.

Why the ritual? Why the symbolism?

And what about the children? Why were they in church? Shouldn't they be in Sunday school for the whole time — dropped off by their parents before the adults went to church?

One Sunday, the priest announced the need for additional Sunday readers. If anyone believed they could serve God in this way, they were asked to speak with him.

At that time, my son was four years old. He was obviously struck by the invitation, because after the service he said that he would like to read in church the following Sunday. The priest tried to explain that there were lots of big words in the

Bible and that he'd never had a child volunteer to read before. "Maybe," the priest said, "you might like to wait a bit before tackling such a big job."

"No, thank you," my son cheerfully replied. "I'll practice lots with Mommy. I can read the first lesson, and go to Sunday school right after. So I won't miss too much. Would that help you out, Reverend Jack?"

I really don't think the priest knew what had hit him. Could the child actually read? He'd never had a child read the lessons during a Sunday service before. How would it be received by the congregation?

I assured the priest that my son had been reading since he was two-and-a-half-years old and would have little difficulty reading the Sunday lesson. "But," I wondered, "why would he want to stand up in front of people he hardly knows and read the Bible?"

My son's answer was clear. "Reverend Jack needs help. I can help."

I'd heard the same invitation for Sunday readers. With a background in radio and television, I knew I had a pleasant voice and could articulate well. Yet I wasn't ready to help in any way which might include standing up and being visible in church. I wanted to be inconspicuous.

The next Sunday, my son stood on the chancel steps. The Bible was larger than his hands could easily hold. As he began with the words, "A reading from . . . ," his voice was strong. He read well — enunciating clearly and with meaning, speaking slowly and loud enough for all to hear.

The word of God was proclaimed that day by a four-year-old child who seemed to be light-years ahead of his mother in understanding what it meant to serve God.

Reflection Starters Two

When was the first time you were aware of God "disturbing" your life?

How did you respond? Record some of your recollections in your Prayer Journal.

As you prayerfully reflect on that event, circumstance, incident, moment, what insight do you now have?

- Take a moment to sit in silence.
- Invite the Holy Spirit to breathe, within you, an awareness of God's special love for you.

Have you ever ignored what may have been an invitation to serve God? Reflect on that incident in your Prayer Journal.

Chapter Three

A year later, when my son was five years old, he said, "Mommy, tell me the story of my baptism."

The children from the Sunday school had come into the church for an infant baptism that morning. My son was curious about his own baptism and wanted to know when and where it had occurred, if he had cried, who was there . . .

"There's no story to tell," I replied. "You've never been baptized."

"Why not?" he asked.

"Well, I thought that I'd wait until you were old enough to make your own decision."

"I'm old enough now," he said.

I tried gently to change the subject, but he continued. "Mommy, I want to be baptized."

"Let's talk about this when you're older."

"When will that be?" he queried.

"How about when you're six?"

"Six? I'm ready now. Why do I have to wait?"

Good question. I didn't have an answer. So I simply replied, "We'll see." I was beginning to feel uneasy. First the Bible Study. Now my son wanted to be baptized.

What was going on? God was breaking into my life, "disturbing" it, for the second time. Only I didn't recognize it.

Reflection Starters Three

Name and reflect on some of the major events of your life. Was any a moment when God "disturbed" your life?

Did that disturbance occur through
- a friend?
- a situation?
- a decision?
- a family member?

Take some time to prayerfully remember the incident.

In your Prayer Journal, reflect on some of the specifics of the disturbance. For example
- What was said and who said it?
- What was done and who did it?
- What was your reaction at the time?

Chapter Four

After worship the following Sunday, I noticed my son chatting with the priest. In a few minutes, the priest approached me saying, "It seems I've been invited to tea this coming Saturday, to discuss your son's baptism. Would two o'clock be convenient?"

How could I gracefully get out of having the priest to tea to talk about my son's baptism, especially when I wasn't sure that it was something I wanted for my child?

Saturday came. My son was expectantly waiting for the visit. It was definitely a highlight of his day. It was definitely a stress point of my day. How could I explain that I didn't know what baptism meant? How could I express my concern that my son was too young to choose to become an Anglican?

When the priest arrived, I decided to let him know my feelings. I asked lots of questions and was pleasantly surprised to hear the simple answers.

"Baptism," he explained, "is simply the church's way of welcoming someone into God's family."

"In baptism," continued the priest, "one is formally received as a Christian. The denomination may be chosen later if the person chooses to restate the baptismal vows at a special service of Confirmation or Affirmation."

By agreeing to my son's baptism, I was supporting his obvious desire to publicly join God's family. I wasn't making him become a member of a particular denomination.

Throughout the discussion in our backyard, my son sometimes listened attentively, and sometimes scampered off to play. The priest explained that it was his practice to baptize infants during the main Sunday service, and children and adults in the afternoons, privately.

That suited me just fine! A shy person by nature, I didn't want to be up front in church on a Sunday morning. A private afternoon baptism was perfect. But something caused my son to return just as we were discussing which Sunday afternoon would be most convenient to have the baptism.

"Reverend Jack, why can't I be baptized in the morning?" he asked.

The priest was obviously surprised at this request and replied, "Well, it's possible, but I've never baptized anyone but babies during a Sunday service."

"Why not? I want God's family there. I want them to welcome me. Just like when babies are baptized."

The priest mulled this over, thinking out loud. "Well . . ."

My son's voice broke into his thoughts. "Reverend Jack, you don't have to carry me up the aisle. Not like the babies. You could just hold my hand!"

And with those words, he ran off to play on the swing set. A few weeks later, after my son was baptized during a Sunday morning service, he walked up the aisle holding Reverend Jack's hand and greeting his new family.

Reflection Starters Four

Think of a time when another person was used by God to bring you to a decision. In your Prayer Journal, describe the incident. Who was involved? What was your decision?

When did you realize God was involved in the decision-making process?

Have you ever let that individual know she or he was used by God in your spiritual journey? If not, consider doing so — in person, by letter, by phone.

If you cannot share their involvement in your faith journey with them, consider offering this prayer of thanksgiving.

> Loving Creator,
> you have often been present in my life,
> guiding me and putting in my path
> those who would be a catalyst
> for the next step in my journey with you.
> I especially gives thanks for . . . . (name)
> who . . . . (be specific).
> May [he or she] be truly blessed in [his or her] faith journey.
> This I ask in the name of your Son, Jesus Christ,
> who has been the catalyst for countless searchers
> over the centuries. Amen.

Chapter Five

"Mommy, tell me the story of your baptism." It was the evening after my son's baptism, and my five-year-old son, with his innocent question, provided yet another opportunity for God to "disturb" my life.

My baptism? The question was too close for comfort. I was aware of a change in my breathing. Something (Someone?) was disturbing my thoughts, my innermost being. I remembered feeling the same way only two other times — when the priest invited me to Bible Study and when my son asked to be baptized. What was it all about?

This was unsettling and I was hesitant to explore where it might lead. If I dared to open one door, then I might be invited to open another, and another, and another. As these thoughts raced through my mind in an instant, my son lovingly looked at me for an answer.

"Mommy, what is your baptismal story?"

"Baptismal story? I don't have one. I've never been baptized."

"Why not?" asked the innocently challenging voice.

"Well, when I was a little girl, I went to a church that didn't believe in baptism," I explained.

Incredulous, he continued. "But how did you know you were part of God's family?"

"We were told we were," I replied. "Now, how about getting ready for your bath?" I cheerfully added, hoping to change the subject.

Not to be deterred, he continued, "Mommy, what are you afraid of?"

Afraid? I felt, at that moment, as if my soul had been penetrated. I'll never forget his wide-open eyes filled with concern as he stood on the chair, leaned across the table, held my hand, and said, "You know, baptism doesn't hurt."

As I was tucking him into bed that night, he put his small arms around my neck and sleepily said, "Please talk to Reverend Jack and get baptized. It's good to have God's family welcome you."

With those words he closed his eyes and drifted off to sleep, leaving his mother wondering what was going on.

What was going on was yet another disturbance in my life.

Reflection Starters Five

What is your baptismal story?*

- Was it a private baptism?
- During a Sunday morning service?
- Do you have any pictures?
- Who of your family and friends attended?
- Were you baptized as an infant, child, youth, adult?
- Where were you baptized?
- Who baptized you?
- When were you baptized (when was your "baptismal birthday")?

You may discover yourself on an adventure, locating the above facts. It may involve digging through family records, talking with family members, contacting the church. Once you have the facts, note them in your Prayer Journal.

Do you celebrate your baptismal birthday (the day of your spiritual birth)? If so, how? Note some of the celebrations in your Prayer Journal.

Has it been with as much celebration as the celebration of your physical birthday? If not, what might you do to celebrate your next baptismal birthday? Consider some possibilities in your Prayer Journal.

*You may want to refer to the entry on baptism in the Glossary of Terms at the end of this book.

Choices

Choose life so that your descendants may live
— Deuteronomy 30:19

Chapter Six

As I reflected on the possibility of baptism for myself, I discovered that I wasn't overly enthusiastic. I considered myself to be a child of God. Why would I need to be baptized? But as time passed, I sensed a call to obedience. Not a blind, unthinking obedience, but a patient willingness to trust my intuition and let God work in my life.

The word *obedience* is both simple and complex. On the one hand, it is simple to obediently follow what one personally believes to be God's leading. Just say Yes. On the other hand, it is complex to faithfully follow, for faithfulness involves discerning God's will.

I find it helpful to consider both the vertical and horizontal aspects of the Cross when seeking to know God's will. Checking the decision with God is the vertical pillar, and listening to other human beings is the horizontal cross-piece.

In the nine months before I was baptized, I began to learn about faithfully listening and responding to God's call. Whether I felt an emotional response or not!

Good thing, too, for when I was finally baptized, I felt nothing. There was no emotional high, no dramatic sense of God's presence filling my innermost being, no cognitive awareness of God's direction.

There was, however, an indefinable assurance that I had discerned God's will for my life at that time. By my baptism, a symbolic door to my spiritual journey had opened.

Reflection Starters Six

Have you ever considered the element of "obedience" as part of your Christian vocation? In your Prayer Journal, reflect on those moments of your spiritual journey when you were consciously obedient to God's leading.

Reflect on those moments of your spiritual journey when you followed your own desire without discerning God's will. Food for thought might be found in the following:

> Blessed are those who follow their own desire. No one, when tempted, should say "I am being tempted by God; for God cannot be tempted by evil and God tempts no one. But one is tempted by one's own desire, being lured and enticed by that. Then, when that desire has conceived, it gives birth to sin and that sin, when fully grown, gives birth to death. Do not be deceived, my beloved (James 1:12a, 13 –16).

Have you ever experienced God directing you to

- a decision,
- a new awareness,
- a new learning,

without an assurance of emotional confirmation, yet with an inner peace? Take some time to reflect on those moments in your Prayer Journal.

Chapter Seven

The year following my baptism was spent going in and out of doctors' offices. Scar tissue from previous surgery was causing a lot of pain. Additional surgery was performed. But recovery was slow and painful.

I seemed to be getting worse, not better. "Why don't you go on holidays as you planned? That'll help take your mind off the pain," said the physician as he performed the post-operative check-up.

So we set off on our holidays. But within twenty-four hours, I was seriously ill. Complications had arisen. Admitted to hospital for emergency surgery, I was told that my life was in danger. I might not make it through surgery. If I'd not already done so, I should make out my will. Scary news!

The church where I'd been baptized had a prayer group whose members prayed for those who needed help. I needed help and asked for prayer. I gained comfort by the sense that others were upholding me in their prayers. I tried to "let go and let God" take over the entire situation. It wasn't easy.

I started thinking about the many stresses in my life.

- I was seriously ill.
- If I survived surgery, recovery would be lengthy.
- Complete recovery wasn't a certainty.
- My husband wasn't coping well with having a wife who had spent much of the past year in and out of hospitals.

- Our marriage was beginning to experience noticeable tension.
- My son was beginning to reflect the stress of his home environment.

I began to quietly rage at God. My health, my marriage, my son's emotional state — nothing was right. "Where is God?" I wondered.

Reflection Starters Seven

Do you believe that God heals today?

Have you experienced God's healing in your life? —
- healing of relationships,
- healing of addictions,
- healing of attitudes,
- healing of compulsions,
- healing of illness,
- healing of emotions,
- healing of memories.

Reflect on those instances in your Prayer Journal.

Have you ever raged at God? Have you ever wondered "Where is God?" in a particular situation, crisis, or relationship?

Reflect on the situations in your Prayer Journal and what you discovered — or what you have yet to discover.

Chapter Eight

In my search for God, I began to read the Bible. Through Scripture reading, I came to realize that God's presence was with me during the many painful and stress-filled months. I discovered that God ached with me in my physical pain and suffering, God grieved with me for my straining marriage, God agonized with me over my inability to fully care for my son.

In Scripture, I encountered a God who seemed to understand and "be with" me in my wilderness experiences. Through Christ, God had experienced all the pain, grief, and frustration that humanity can know. This was a new-found discovery. And it was consoling. I found that I wanted to know more about this God.

Six long months of physical recovery were spent on the living-room couch. There was lots of time to think, lots of time to pray, lots of time to question.

There was a spiritual ache that I could barely murmur to myself, let alone articulate to another human being. I silently wondered, "If I were to publicly confirm my baptismal promises, stating my desire to become a member of the Anglican church, would I come to know God more deeply?"

The more I considered this possibility, the clearer became the inner encouragement to seek Confirmation. There was an indefinable assurance that I had discerned God's will for my life at that time, and that I was being led to publicly confirm my baptismal vows.

When I knelt before the bishop for Confirmation, I felt no special deepening of my faith, no compulsion to get more deeply involved in the church, no sense that God was directing me — no discernible "voice," that is.

But during the past months, I had come to know that it was right. I was confirmed because I could not do otherwise.

Reflection Starters Eight

Have you ever had a spiritual "ache" that motivated you to consciously search for, and get to know more about, God? Reflect on that search in your Prayer Journal.

If you've formally confirmed your baptismal vows, reflect on that in your Prayer Journal. In other words, what is the story of your Confirmation?*

- Why did you decide to be confirmed?
- Did you have formal Confirmation preparation?
- If so, what did you study or learn in your preparation?
- Who was the priest who presented you for Confirmation?
- Who confirmed you?

*You may want to refer to the entry on Confirmation in the Glossary of Terms at the end of this book.

- Who of your family, friends, baptismal sponsors, attended your Confirmation?
- Do you have a copy of the Confirmation service bulletin, if one was made?
- Any photos?

What do you remember about your Confirmation? Reflect on those memories in your Prayer Journal.

When you confirmed your baptismal promises, what did you understand as the meaning of Confirmation? Note that in your Prayer Journal.

Do you still hold that view? If not, how has it changed? Note the changed view in your Prayer Journal.

If you've not confirmed your baptismal vows, what would encourage you to do so? Note your response in your Prayer Journal.

Chapter Nine

With Confirmation came the call to a deeper commitment to God. "Trust me," I believed God was saying. Easy to say; not easy to do — especially when your life takes another twist. The twist was my son's illness.

Always a bright, active child, he began to develop an inability to concentrate in school. His mind was always busy. His body was so constantly mobile that he couldn't sit still in a classroom or even at the dinner table during a meal.

The family physician said, "Keep him busier!" Over the next year, he enrolled in many extra-curricular activities — cubs, dance classes, library reading program, drama classes, t-ball, soccer, drum classes, swimming lessons. His interest in politics led him to initiate the LPK Club (Little Political Kids), a club for children in the community who were interested in politics. Because of his frustration with the lack of meaningful children's television, he approached the local cable channel and designed his own children's program.

He was busy all right, but it didn't seem to be helping. Before his eighth birthday, he began to exhibit destructive behaviour, low self-esteem, despondency, and depression. The diagnosis was hyperactivity, and the medical solution was, "Let's put him on Ritalin."

What had happened to the outgoing, cheerful, personable, gentle, loving, contented little boy of a year ago? This wasn't the child I knew. Something was causing him to behave the way he did.

We tried medical tests, counselling, and attending special sessions on the gifted child (because we thought that perhaps his intellectual giftedness might be a contributing factor to the change in his personality). We explored any avenue which we thought might be helpful. Insight into the problem was gained, but no solution. And it was a solution we needed!

This period of time was stressful for each of us. My husband and I were confused, angry, and tense. We were disappointed with ourselves because of our seeming inability to cope. Our already strained marriage was deteriorating further. My son experienced his own sense of frustration, anger, and confusion, and continued downhill.

It was at this point that I realized we needed special help. So, I prayed — adding my prayers to those already being offered by special friends.

Reflection Starters Nine

What is your understanding of prayer? Note that in your Prayer Journal.

In your Prayer Journal, reflect on your various experiences of prayer.

One way of praying is to incorporate the ACTS principle; that is

- Adoration (praising God),
- Confession (sharing with God your omissions and commissions of actions, and/or thoughts which separate you from God),
- Thanksgiving (taking time to thank God for the little as well as the big miracles and God-incidences in your life and the world around you),
- Supplication (interceding on behalf of others for their needs).

Consider each of these aspects of prayer in your own devotional time. Is each included daily?

Do you pray on a regular basis? How and when do you pray?

What do you pray about? Take a moment to journal some of your prayers, classifying them according to the ACTS principle of prayer (Adoration, Confession, Thanksgiving, Supplication).

Do you believe God answers prayer?

If so, how? Take a moment to journal your response.

If not, why not? Take a moment to journal your response.

Chapter Ten

As a result of prayer, God reminded me of an earlier experience when my son was an infant and diagnosed with celiac disease. Because of that experience, I was motivated to take a holistic approach to illness, combining nutrition, prayer, and medication.

But where to begin this time? God's prompting seemed to lead me to the library and the local health food store. Eventually, from my reading and study, three important facts became apparent.

- Refined sugar and chocolate could cause symptoms similar to my son's.

- Salicylate-sensitivity and additive or preservative reactions were possible causes in hyperkinetic and hyperactive behavior.

- A link between food sensitivity and chemical or mineral imbalance had been scientifically recognized.

Because of these facts, I began to lose conviction in the efficacy of using Ritalin alone. A physician who specialized in preventive medicine suggested that food sensitivity might be a cause. By eliminating certain food substances, we might see a marked improvement in my son's behavior, self-image, and ability to concentrate.

It was Hallowe'en. On the long ride home, my son and I chatted about the physician's recommendation. I asked him whether he liked feeling the way he'd been feeling, and doing the destructive things he'd been doing.

"No, I don't. I don't know why I do those things. I know they're not right, but I can't stop," he sobbed.

"Would you like to stop?" I gently queried. "Would you like to feel better?"

"Yes," he muttered quietly, trying to hold back the tears.

"Well, there are a couple of things we could try," I replied, praying for God's words as I spoke.

"The doctor thinks that your body doesn't like certain foods and that, when you eat those foods, your body and mind react, making your head fuzzy and your body do things it shouldn't do. If we take those things out of your diet, you'll probably begin to feel better, think more clearly, and not be so naughty. Would you like to try it?"

There was a long silence as he considered what I'd said. "What things would I have to give up? When would I start?" he queried.

"It won't be easy. You'd have to eliminate all things that have sugar, chocolate, white flour, additives, preservatives, and salicylates in them. And if you're going to try this, it might be a good idea to begin right away."

More silence. We were almost home. I wondered what was going on in his little head. But I knew enough that, if we were to try the nutritional approach, he would have to be in favour of it, otherwise it wouldn't work.

"Does God know it's Hallowe'en, and that I go out trick-or-treating and get lots of candies and stuff?"

Does God know? What a strange question, I thought. "What do you mean?" I queried.

"I don't like God very much if I'm supposed to give up the fun of trick-or-treating. Maybe I'll start this thing tomorrow, so I can still have fun tonight."

"Well, you can begin tomorrow, but do you really want to wait? If your body can't handle sugar and chocolate, how would you feel tomorrow morning if you ate that stuff tonight?"

"Yucky," he sniffed in response. "I really don't like God very much today," he continued. After a lengthy silence, he said resignedly, "Okay. I'll start now. But I sure hope this works!"

"Good for you," I proudly replied. "Now, how about you go out trick-or-treating with your friends tonight. When you come home, I'll have some treats for you that you'll be able to eat. They'll be on your new diet. I'll exchange what you've collected with what I've made. How does that sound?"

"That sounds good," he said with a reluctant smile on his face.

It sounded good, but I really didn't know what I was going to do about making treats to exchange for his goodies when he returned home. So, I prayed, once again, for God's direction.

Reflection Starters Ten

Have you ever asked others to pray for you?

- What motivated you?
- How did you feel?
- What was the outcome?

Reflect on the occasion(s) in your Prayer Journal.

If you've never asked someone else to pray for you, what might have contributed to that decision? To your reluctance? Reflect on this in your Prayer Journal.

Have you ever experienced God encouraging you into an action or a decision which you'd rather not do, yet sensed God's leading? Reflect on that experience in your Prayer Journal.

What is your understanding of God's existence in the midst of suffering? Reflect on that understanding in your Prayer Journal.

Have you ever "not liked God"? Reflect on the occasion(s) in your Prayer Journal.

Stillness

Be still before the Lord and wait patiently
— Psalm 37:7

Chapter Eleven

I'd been discovering that God wants to speaks to us, wants to guide our day. But distracted by the busyness of our lives, the stresses of our home, work, or school situations, our inability to "be still" and seek God's guidance, we often aren't able to listen.

I knew I needed God's guidance; so I went into my "prayer chamber" — the bathtub. When stressed, warm water relaxes me and I can "be still and know that God is God."

Soon I felt God's peace flow within me and sensed God's direction. If I consulted the owner of the health food store, I'd know how to exchange wholesome food for tricks-and-treats! That Hallowe'en evening was great fun in our home, as the "yucky" goodies were replaced by interestingly different treats sweetened with rice syrup and natural fruit juices.

"Mommy, I think that God wants me to really work on this new diet." God again! How was it that God spoke so clearly to my child and so obtusely to me?

My son continued. "Derek's birthday party is coming up. There'll be ice-cream and cake at the party. And what about cub camp? We always have hot dogs, but they have nitrite in them. Can you make me things I can eat instead?

"Don't worry about it. I'll figure something out," I answered, not really sure what I'd do.

I began to experiment. Some experiments were wonderful successes; others were incredible flops. Eventually, out of rice flour, I made something that looked like a cupcake. Along with this and goat's-milk ice-cream from the local health food store, my son was able to go to the birthday party and eat his treats.

By the time of cub camp at the end of the summer — where, according to my son, everyone "pigged out" on hot dogs — whole-wheat hot dog buns were ready to go with the nitrite-free hot dogs. I was grateful for the words in Scripture, "Ask and it shall be given unto you," which encouraged me to seek help from the local baker and butcher.

Through all this, the change in my son was dramatic! Less than seventy-two hours after we began the new diet, the fidgets and tension at the table were gone and we could once again have a relaxed meal. Soon the school reported that his level of concentration was improving; his low self-image began to rise. The happy child I once knew was again emerging.

Gratitude for his newly recovered health led him to suggest that we share with others what we had discovered because, he reminded me, "God teaches us to share." So I designed and began leading nutritional workshops for parents of hyperactive children. At each class I was asked for my cookbook — a cookbook which didn't exist in reality, or even in thought!

But slowly, a cookbook for people who couldn't tolerate refined sugar, additives, chocolate, preservatives, refined flour, or salicylates took shape. I prayed it would meet some specific needs of readers and generate an excitement to explore areas of nutrition and wholeness in body, mind, and spirit.

Letters from cookbook readers around the world indicated that my prayers were being answered. God does, indeed, move in wonderful and mysterious ways!

Reflection Starters Eleven

Do you have a prayer chamber, a special place where you can be still with God? Where is it?

- a special chair?
- your bathtub?
- your bed?
- your patio?
- your car?
- some cushions?
- a prayer-kneeler?
- a rock overlooking the ocean?
- a particular place in your home you've made sacred?

What makes your prayer chamber sacred? Reflect on that in your Prayer Journal.

God invites us to share, to be stewards. In what ways has your life been a life of faithful stewardship?

- stewardship of creation?
- stewardship of knowledge?
- stewardship of resources?
- stewardship of gifts and talents?
- stewardship of love?
- stewardship of finances?
- stewardship of creativity?
- stewardship of wisdom?
- stewardship of physical abilities?

Consider each of these in your Prayer Journal.

When was the last time you were aware of God's moving "in wonderful and mysterious ways" in your life?

Spend some quiet time reflecting on that experience, that moment, that awareness in your Prayer Journal.

Chapter Twelve

God was entering my awareness more and more often. Bible Study, conferences, regular attendance at church, reading devotional books. I truly hungered to know more about God.

One Christmas Eve, casually reading material on the church's bulletin board, I noticed a flyer about a nearby theological school. Over the Christmas holidays, I read the material and realized that I could study about God, get a master's degree while doing it, and prepare myself for employment as a Christian educator, building on my previous experience as a high school teacher.

Christmas, the worldwide celebration of the birthing time for Christianity was, that year, a new birthing time for me!

Accepted into the Master of Theological Studies (MTS) program to prepare for my goal of becoming a parish Christian educator, I enthusiastically applied myself to the classes, reading, and required papers. My husband and son enthusiastically supported this new endeavour and took pride in the encouraging comments professors wrote on my papers.

How exciting and stimulating it all was! Biblical studies opened up the Bible in ways I'd never before encountered. Ministry courses enlarged my understanding of ministry. History and Theology courses broadened my overview of the church. Denominational studies introduced me to the wonders and curiosities of Anglicanism. Daily worship fed my soul. It was difficult to remember when I'd encountered learning that was so fulfilling. Each day, each course, each opportunity was new, refreshing, and challenging!

But it wasn't long before God disturbed my life again, this time through the questioning voice of faculty and other students. "Why aren't you in the Master of Divinity program?" they asked. That was easy to answer. The Master of Divinity degree prepared candidates for ordination, and I sensed no call to ordination.

"Ordination is for men, not women," I thought. I was using a "Jeremiah type" of excuse — "Ah, Lord God! I do not know how . . . for I am only a youth" (Jeremiah 1:6). My experience in the Anglican church had been only of male clergy. My Jeremiah excuse was that I was a woman.

My reading of Scripture seemed to support this view. But biblical studies were beginning to shed new light on the matter, as were the numerous women of various denominations who were preparing themselves for ordained ministry, and the male students who were encouragingly supportive of the ordination of women.

Being open to a call to ordination wasn't easy. I pushed the possibility into my subconscious and continued in the Master of Theological Studies program. But God disturbed my life again in a brief encounter with my bishop at a special parish anniversary celebration.

When I was introduced to him as a student in the Master of Theological Studies program, he smiled and said, "The MTS program? Have you ever considered the possibility of ordination?" With that question, he walked away, leaving me balancing a tea cup that was beginning to shake.

The possibility of ordination. There were those words again. I knew that I would have to begin exploring such a possibility, even though I couldn't hear God calling me to such a ministry.

"Can't I serve as a Christian educator?" I prayed. No response. "Why me?" I implored. No response. Just a deepening sense of being led to open the door to the possibility of ordination.

Reflection Starters Twelve

Recall times in your life when God called you to serve in a particular way, but you set up your own Jeremiah excuse; for example,

- sharing your faith with another at work or school;
- witnessing to your friends
  - by saying that Sunday morning is when you go to church and you don't get involved in other Sunday morning events,
  - by inviting them to join you at church and then brunch after the Sunday service;
- serving in the church
  - as an intercessor, altar guild member, choir member, Sunday school teacher, prayer chain member, committee member, and so on.

In your Prayer Journal, record times in your life when you allowed Jeremiah excuses to deter you from serving God in a particular way.

What, in your opinion, should be the requirements for ordination?

Are there any categories of people you feel should not be ordained? Why? Reflect on this in your Prayer Journal. . . .

Do you know how God "called" your parish priest, deacon, bishop? Invite them to tell you their spiritual story.

Have you ever hungered to know more about God? How have you satiated that hunger?

Have you ever experienced worship as "feeding your soul"? In your Prayer Journal, reflect on a particular occasion when worship was rich, meaningful, and fed your soul. Consider what elements contributed to that experience.

Chapter Thirteen

One day, the bishop came to the theological college to meet the Anglican students. He was not only our diocesan bishop, but also the archbishop with pastoral oversight of all Anglican students from his ecclesiastical province (a division based on diocesan boundaries, not on political boundaries).

To those who had gathered and indicated they were not sponsored for ordination by any bishop, he said, "I don't know what plans you have, but if you're open to the possibility of ordination, wait behind and I'll explain the process to you."

Here it was again, the "possibility" of ordination! My heart began to accelerate and my mouth went dry. Somehow I found my body moving towards the group of students that were gathering around the archbishop, as he explained the process which included psychological tests, appearing before ACPO (Advisory Committee on Postulants for Ordination), parish support, and final meeting with the archbishop.

"Which of you wants to begin the process towards the possibility of ordination?" he asked.

"Not me," I wanted to shout, but instead, heard myself giving my name so that I could be placed on the list for the psychological tests.

I thought, "Okay God, I'll write those tests. They'll show that I'm not suited for ordained ministry."

Several weeks later, those who had written the psychological tests were met by the archbishop who, in a personal interview, gave each one a synopsis of the psychologist's report.

"You are called to be a priest, June. The tests strongly indicate this," I heard him say. My thoughts were jumbled. I had so many questions, so much to assimilate.

The archbishop continued. "I want you to go to ACPO. There your call to the priesthood will be further tested by representatives of the Anglican Communion. They will report to me, and then we'll see where we go from there."

So much for thinking I knew what God intended for my life!

Reflection Starters Thirteen

Have you ever thought you knew what God intended for your life, only to discover later that you hadn't clearly heard? Reflect on that experience in your Prayer Journal.

What "possibilities" of spiritual growth has God put before you?

How did you respond? Note your response in your Prayer Journal.

Chapter Fourteen

The decision was made and I began working toward ordination. But in the meantime, once again, my son became ill. This time he experienced dizziness, weakness, nausea, lethargy, and an inability to grow physically. Such strange symptoms.

School took all his energy. He was no longer able to attend and enjoy his extracurricular activities. Some days he was too weak even to attend school. Strange physical symptoms began to appear in the rest of our family, including Muffin, our cat.

We wondered what might have caused this change of health in our family. Was there something in our home to which we were allergic? The only new thing was the installation of UFFI (Urea Formaldehyde Foam Insulation), a supposedly safe, dependable, and relatively inexpensive product.

Might that be our problem? I decided to play detective. That afternoon, I packed up my son and went to visit a nearby friend. He lay on her couch while we talked. In about two hours, he got up from the couch and asked if he could go out to play with his friends.

Out he went — pasty-colored face, thin little body — to play. A miracle had just happened!

Slowly his energy began to return, and he seemed to be enjoying himself. I thought, "He's been away from the UFFI-filled house for a couple of hours. Can that be the reason for his newly found energy?"

There was only one way to tell — take him home. So home we went. It wasn't long before I found him on his bed, listlessly staring at the ceiling, "I don't feel very well," he said quietly.

That evening my husband and I considered our options. We needed to have more substantive evidence that our home was causing the reactions. For the next few days, my son and I visited our neighbour. After a few hours in her home, his lethargy again dissipated. "Is it psychological?" we wondered.

But our cat continued to throw up her meals, my husband continued to have eye problems, I continued to experience nausea, my son continued to lack energy and lose weight.

One night, I checked into a local motel with my son. He was so weak that he had to be carried into the car and into the motel. Even the novelty of being in a motel for the first time didn't arouse him from lethargy. He was glad to be in bed and soon drifted off to sleep.

How I prayed that night! Soon I, too, fell asleep.

"This is fun! A motel, wow! Can we eat in the restaurant? Can I order whatever I want? How about pancakes and . . ." With those words I was awakened early the next morning by an energetic little boy, bouncing on the bed!

If I wanted proof, this was it! He had been out of the house for more than twelve hours and was himself once again. "Alleluia!" I phoned my husband at work where he was just coming off of a night shift. "It's the UFFI. We need to talk about where we go from here," I said.

Where we went from there was an immediate decision to demolish the house and move into temporary lodgings. The severity of my son's reaction indicated that trying to remove the UFFI wouldn't suffice. It could not be completely eliminated from the wires and wooden frame of the house.

Demolish one home, design another, find a place to live while the contractor built our new home, choose carpeting and paint colour and kitchen cabinets, pack the house contents for storage, move to temporary housing, be with my son when he woke up each morning and at the neighbor's each afternoon when he returned from school.

All this, and write papers and tests, and attend classes at college, as well as deal with a marriage whose problems escalated. The stress was incredible!

Yet somehow, there was a deep peace. Through it all I was aware of a miracle surrounding my son's health. We had discovered the cause of his illness and it was curable. There was much for which to be thankful.

Reflection Starters Fourteen

Do you believe in miracles?

In your Prayer Journal, reflect on your understanding of miracles

- in Jesus' time,
- in today's society,
- in your life.

Have you ever experienced great stress or been "in crisis" while experiencing a profound sense of unexplainable peace? Reflect on that experience in your Prayer Journal.

Chapter Fifteen

Friends, students, and faculty at the theological college were aware of the crises that I was facing at home. I had to do my assignments, attend most classes, share in the arrangements for the demolition of the house, move to temporary lodgings, plan the new house, and spend time each day with my son. But at the same time, I was strangely able to remain peaceful.

One day, a faculty member asked me into the office. I thought it was to discuss a paper I'd recently submitted, but was surprised to discover the purpose of the meeting. "June, we've all been aware of the crises in your family. But I'm curious. What keeps you so peaceful, and how are you able to cope?" Apparently a number of people had been wondering the same thing.

Surely this person knew that such peace came from Christ and that I was able to cope by God's grace. I wondered if this were an invitation to witness. But I didn't know how to witness, how to express my faith, how to evangelize.

I remembered reading, somewhere, that evangelism is simply "sharing one's faith with another in a variety of ways." And I recalled a time when my husband and I were experiencing increased marital difficulties. A friend sensed my spiritual unease and wrote a note which read,

My friend, you are not alone. I am with you in prayer. Even if you don't feel like going to church, go to church.

Even if you don't think you're getting anything out of the service, go to church. Go and be surrounded by the prayers of others, and know that God is God. This time will pass and, one day, you will know that God has been with you. You are not alone.

This was a powerful witness of one person's faith — evangelism pure and simple! All I needed to do was to remember to be a KISS theologian (Keep It Simple, Sweetheart).

With a profound awareness of God's presence in that office, I began to share how I'd personally experienced the peace of Christ in the midst of pain, suffering, and family crises, and how I had gained a personal experience of the presence of Jesus Christ in my life.

Together we prayed. And as we prayed, I became aware that God was using me to bring another to a deeper relationship with Christ. I was humbled by such a precious opportunity and privilege.

God was becoming more and more integrated with every part of my life and my very being. Another opportunity to be thankful!

Reflection Starters Fifteen

Have you ever been used by God, that you know of, to lead another to a deeper awareness of Christ in their life? Reflect on that experience in your Prayer Journal.

Reflecting on the phrase, "Ask and you shall receive," consider a particular time when you asked God for something specific. In your Prayer Journal, reflect on how God answered that prayer, keeping in mind that God can respond with No or Yes or Not yet.

How would you define "evangelism"?

Have you ever "witnessed" to another of your belief in Jesus Christ? Reflect on that occasion in your Prayer Journal.

Life

I have come that they may have life
and have it abundantly

— John 10:10

Chapter Sixteen

As the years went by, my marriage deteriorated to the point of despair. I often found myself wondering about a God who, on the one hand, would lead me into marriage (through which I would be introduced to the joy of Christian fellowship, baptism, Confirmation, discovery of biblical truths, profound experience of prayer, daily experience of God's love for me) and, on the other hand, would end the marriage in divorce.

What kind of a God would have me experience such pain? The words of St Paul, "in weakness there is strength," came to have special meaning during this time of marital turmoil.

When it seemed there was no possibility of reconciliation, I went to my bishop to explain, in confidence, the difficulty of my crumbling marriage. In less than a year, my studies would be over. Would he ordain someone who was divorced? Was he still supportive of my call to the priesthood?

His response surprised me, "Divorce, in your situation, seems the healthy option."

"I thought the church was against divorce," I countered.

"As Christians," he said, "we are invited to choose life. By remaining in your marriage, which is unhealthy for many reasons, you are not choosing life, either for yourself or your son."

"Sometimes," he explained, "like a surgeon who cuts the

skin to remove a cancer, one needs to cut a marriage to remove a cancerous relationship."

Before I could ask him whether he would still sponsor me for ordination, he continued, "As for ordination, I ordain the person who I believe has a call to the priesthood. I do not ordain one's marital status. I believe you do have a call to the priesthood, and I expect you to continue your studies."

I left the bishop's office, curious about the seeming contradictions between Christian Scripture and practice, and full of wonder and gratitude at the operation of God's grace in the midst of it all.

Reflection Starters Sixteen

Are there circumstances in which you believe God would be supportive of a decision to divorce? Consider some of those circumstances in your Prayer Journal.

If you knew that a priest were divorced, would that have a bearing on your consideration of that person for employment in your parish? Why? Why not?

If you knew that a candidate for bishop were divorced, would that have a bearing on your consideration of that person for election as bishop in your diocese? Why? Why not?

Reflect on these responses in your Prayer Journal.

Have you ever been aware of moments in your life when "in weakness" there has been "strength"? Reflect on those moments in your Prayer Journal.

Do you believe that God *allows* pain and suffering? Do you believe that God *causes* pain and suffering?

In your Prayer Journal, reflect on your understanding of God's role in pain and suffering.

Chapter Seventeen

With those pastoral words from my bishop, I began to "choose life" (as the Deuteronomist wrote in the Old Testament) for myself and my son. The marriage was dissolved.

But more difficulties lay ahead of us. With the ending of a financially stable suburban life, a new way of living became our reality. We moved into residence on campus. Our studio-like, one-bedroom campus apartment was claustrophobic and confining. Neither of us had much privacy.

My son was entering adolescence and, at a time when he most needed a strong male influence in his life, there was none. He rebelled in every way. School wasn't "challenging" him; life was "the pits." He began to withdraw from everything.

Emotionally we'd been on a roller coaster for several years. With the move out of our home (where my son had his own bedroom and could have his cat with him) and away from our neighborhood (leaving behind friends he'd known most of his life), he experienced further emotional stress and confusion.

His behaviour problems, depression, and school avoidance led us to seek professional help. It seemed important to look for someone who identified him- or her-self as Christian, someone who would be able, not only to use analytical and psychological skills and resources, but also to approach our situation prayerfully.

Such a person was found. He had excellent professional credentials and was a practicing Christian in the Anglican tradition. Books in his office on the healing ministry of the church confirmed the appropriateness of my selection. But, over time, regular visits with him seemed to be going nowhere, and he suggested that my son undergo evaluation from other professionals.

I thought, "Anything that can help explain his downward spiral and move him towards wholeness once again needs to be tried." So my son underwent an evaluation away from home. In the meantime, I tried to focus on my theological schooling and field placement in a parish. Each day I visited him and eagerly awaited those days when he had a day-pass, so that we could once again be together without our every move being evaluated.

Then came the day when the evaluations were complete and a professional recommendation was made. "Your son will need institutionalization, probably for the rest of his life. There is no hope that he'll ever be able to function as a contributing member of society." *What?* I knew he needed help. But, really, institutionalization? For the rest of his life?

The professional continued. "There is only one place that I'd recommend, and that's in the United States." *Was I dreaming?* This was my son he was condemning to a place thousands of miles away.

"Where is your hope?" I shouted. "You say you're a Christian. Christians believe in hope!"

Reflection Starters Seventeen

Have you ever experienced financial distress? How did you react and respond?

In your Prayer Journal, reflect on the experience and your response to that situation. If you have not had this experience, imagine how you would react and respond.

If you did experience financial distress, how were your daily needs (not desires) met? In your Prayer Journal, reflect on how that occurred and where God was in the situation.

If you have not had this experience, imagine yourself in the situation.

What is your understanding of Christian "hope"?

Has there been a situation in your life (or in the life of a loved one or close friend) when others said or indicated that it was hopeless? Reflect on that situation in your Prayer Journal.

What was your response? What was the other's response?

In your Prayer Journal, reflect on the situations and the responses.

Chapter Eighteen

I was devastated. I felt betrayed. I began to identify with Jesus' raging question, "My God, my God, why have you forsaken me?" My mind, body, emotions, spirit were unable to fathom the extent of this pronouncement.

No hope? Surely in God's world, there is always hope!

As I began to assess the situation, I realized that I needed at least to entertain the option of institutionalization, as the doctor had suggested. If it would help my son, then whether I liked the idea or not, I needed to consider it.

"Trust me," I heard God say within my spirit. "Believe in me."

"Yes, God, I do trust you. I believe. But — help my unbelief!"

And God did! As I grew in my trust of God, I sensed a divine encouragement to cease pursuing the alternative of institutionalization for my son.

When I graduated from theological college, we moved off campus into a small two-bedroom apartment near the parish where I was to begin my curacy. My son and I were together, and I experienced a profound awareness of God's presence, even in the midst of my child's escalating emotional and inappropriate behavioural responses.

His continuing refusal to attend school was a major problem. He was intellectually gifted, but he wasn't managing the social aspect of a formal education and was bored with the curriculum. My background as a teacher led me to wonder if I might be able to help him get his high school equivalency.

Home tutoring began. For a few weeks, things went fairly well. But then his depression began again, and he refused to do his assignments, see a physician, or get counselling.

He began sleeping in during the day, and roaming the apartment and streets at night. He became angry, rebellious, and destructive. His behavior was intolerable, and I let him know — as lovingly yet as firmly as possible.

"What are you going to do? Kick me out of here?" he shouted belligerently. "You can't do that. There are laws to protect minors. You're stuck with me, like it or not!"

For much of each day, as an ordained person, I listened to people in turmoil and conflict, praying for, and with, them for a sense of God's presence in their lives. But when I returned to our apartment (my office space, as well as our family space), there was incredible turmoil and conflict.

Daily I sought God's peace and presence in our home. I was grateful that our apartment had been blessed, when we first moved in, by the priest from the parish where I served as the curate.

My son's emotional distress escalated whenever he ate junk food. There were many days when I sat on the floor behind my bedroom door, bracing myself against the wall as he tried to force his way into my room and physically confront me. Whenever he thought I was being too strict, he'd respond by pounding on the walls and screaming as loudly as he could.

Then would come the deafening silence, periods when he'd lock himself into his room, which he'd darkened with tin foil over the windows and blankets stuffed under the door. He would come out of his room only at night to get something to eat. He was frequently out of control in the living room or holed up in his bedroom for days at a time. Unresponsive. Uncommunicative. Unpredictable.

How grateful I was, each Sunday, to hear prayers offered by the people of the parish I served. While it was generic prayer, offered quickly along with prayers for our priest, I took comfort from the belief that God knew my needs and those of my son.

One day, when he was more communicative than usual (he hadn't been able to find any money in my room to buy junk food), I told him that he would have to make a choice — live at home and abide by the house rules, or leave home.

It was his choice.

Reflection Starters Eighteen

Have you ever experienced despair in your life, such that you identified with Christ's cry from the Cross, "My God, my God, why have you forsaken me?" Reflect on that time in your Prayer Journal.

How did God respond to you in that situation? In your Prayer Journal, prayerfully consider God's response.

Have you ever needed "proof" to help your "unbelief," even though, at a conscious level, you believed in God? Reflect on one such instance in your Prayer Journal.

Does your parish pray for its clergy each Sunday? Do you include him or her (or them) in your daily prayers?

- If so, how do you pray for her or him (or them)?
- Consider asking your clergy how you might uphold her or him or them in your prayers.

How does your parish (and how do you) support the ministry of your clergy? Consider raising this issue with your wardens, parish council, church committee, vestry.

Have you ever had your house or apartment blessed? If so, recollect the event in your Prayer Journal. For example,

- Who was there?
- What was said / done?

Then reflect, in your Prayer Journal, on how you have experienced your home since that blessing. Has it made a difference? How?

If you have not had your home blessed, consider discussing this possibility with your priest and perhaps asking her or him to raise the subject in a sermon or inquirer's class.

Chapter Nineteen

"You're throwing me out. I knew you would. So much for loving me!" he screamed.

But I did love him. I loved him enough to be tough and strict and consistent. I explained the house rules once again — get counselling, do your home studies, avoid junk food, observe regular hours of sleep. He responded by grabbing his jacket and saying, "If I can't live here, I'll go live downtown on the streets."

My worst nightmare! But, somehow, I felt God's peace and continued, "If you don't think you can live in this house and abide by the rules, then you're welcome to leave. But I am not throwing you out. You are making the choice. Which piece of luggage would you like to use, the brown or the green?" I thought that would certainly call his bluff and make him see how serious I was.

"I'll take the brown," he shouted and stormed into his room, hurling clothing and stuffed animals into the suitcase.

"I love you," I heard myself quietly reply. "I don't know how to let you know that so you'll really believe it. I know you've had some hurts in your life. You've had a lot of sickness. You hate it when you can't eat a hot dog or candy bar like other kids do. But you can't spend your life running from your problems. And I'm not one of your problems. I'm here for you, when you are ready to come home and observe the house rules."

He listened to what I said, then muttered something

under his breath — and left.

It was a miserably cold and rainy February night. Where was he going? He had no money, just a bus pass that was good only till the end of the month.

In an instant he was gone. Fourteen, very small for his age, hurting, angry, and vulnerable — ever so vulnerable. Into the dark, rainy, and desolate night.

Alone.

Reflection Starters Nineteen

What is your worst nightmare, when it comes to your loved ones?

Should that nightmare come to pass, how could you become aware of God's peace in the midst of the trauma?

Do you think that you would be able to share with others who might be able to uphold you in prayer should your nightmare become reality?

If so, what personal risks might be involved in such transparency and vulnerability?

If you don't think you could share that burden with a sister or brother in Christ, reflect in your Prayer Journal

- Why that might be so;
- What would be necessary for you to allow yourself to be vulnerable with others.

Chapter Twenty

Alone? Not really. God was with him. It was that assurance that got me through the night.

I fully expected he'd return the next morning. But he didn't. Not that night, or the next, or the next, or the next. Finally, late on the fifth night after his stormy departure, I heard the key in the door. "I'm home," came a quiet voice. "Can I come in?"

How to let him know that I loved him, that he was welcome home, yet still let him know that nothing had changed and that he would have to abide by the house rules were he to stay? "Yes, you can come in — that is, if you're ready to follow the rules of the house."

"But I'm cold. And hungry," he said.

"I can see that, but before you come in, I need to know for both our sakes if you're really ready to work at this."

Silence. We looked at each other for what seemed an interminably long time. Then he slowly said, "Tell me again what I have to do."

What I wanted to do was enfold him in my arms and "make it all right" for this child I had carried in my body for over nine months. But I was the adult in the situation and knew that, in order for him to ever have a chance at adulthood, he had to understand that certain consequences followed improper choices.

I quickly offered a silent "arrow prayer" to God for direction and heard myself say, "You've taken the first step. You're open to working on our relationship. While I get you something to eat, why don't you go take a nice hot bath. We'll talk about it over some dinner."

"Okay" he mumbled. "Thanks."

"I'm glad you're home," I gently said. "I've missed you."

It took a lot of work — and time — but in the next several months, there were some remarkable changes. My son agreed to avoid all junk food, go to bed by 11:00 p.m. and get up by 8:00 a.m., become involved as a volunteer in the community, do specific chores in the apartment, and write at least a page each day on a given topic to develop his writing and vocabulary skills.

In time, his diet improved, his sleeping pattern changed, and he became involved in the community as a volunteer in a Teen Crisis Line.

Television and printed news became his hobby. He voraciously read the daily newspaper and watched the news on television each day. This greatly increased his vocabulary and ability to express his feelings and thoughts about many subjects on paper. The daily writing assignments I gave him expanded his horizons. He became a keen researcher, rediscovered the wonders of the local library, and investigated the challenging world of computers.

Over time, he became a prolific and published writer and journalist as well as a proficient self-taught computer programmer.

I remembered the professional's opinion — that my son would never become a contributing member of society — and reflected on the healing which had profoundly affected our lives. I was deeply grateful to God.

Reflection Starters Twenty

An "arrow prayer" could be described as a spur-of-the-moment prayer that simply says, "God, help!" Have you ever offered such a silent prayer to God?

- What were some of those instances?
- What was the situation which initiated such a prayer?
- What was God's response?

Reflect on some recent "arrow prayer" situations. In your Prayer Journal, reflect on God's responses.

Trust

In God I trust. I will not be afraid
— Psalm 56:4 & 11

Chapter Twenty-One

Each day, my son's self-confidence grew as he completed the written assignments that I gave him, and gained respect from the community organizations where he volunteered his time.

One day he received a phone call informing him that he had been chosen by the Vancouver Children's Festival to represent them at a special luncheon with the Prince and Princess of Wales, honouring volunteers. This seemed to be critical to his increasing self-esteem. No longer was it just Mom encouraging him and telling him that he had special gifts to offer others. Out of thousands of volunteers, this large organization had chosen him to represent them.

That night, we talked about God's part in our journey through hell. How, looking back on it all, we could see God's guidance and sustenance. We talked about the gifts God had given each of us, and how we had grown in our spiritual journey from our baptism to that night.

Before going to bed, we talked with God. Together we offered our deep appreciation for never being abandoned when we "walked through the valley of death," as the psalmist had written centuries before.

While there were days when I was afraid, I was also aware — not on a cognitive or emotional level, but deeply, indescribably, on a spiritual level — that God was with us.

The prayer said at our baptism, "Sustain them, O Lord, in your Holy Spirit. Give them an inquiring and discerning heart, the courage to will and to persevere," was an incredibly powerful prayer! God had sustained us both, had given us inquiring and discerning hearts, and also the courage to will and persevere. Thanks be to God!

The psalmist wrote, "Be still, and know that I am God." In other words, "Trust me with your life." Perhaps that's what I had been doing, by God's grace. Sometimes consciously, sometimes without even knowing it.

Strengthened by the baptismal prayers and edified by the prayers of others, I was enabled to trust God. In my spiritual journey of learning to trust God, the prayers of others have been pivotal.

- The prayers of the people offered each Sunday in parishes where I've served (while generic in nature rather than specific) uplifted my spirit on days when it was low.

- The prayers of family and friends (who prayed for specific concerns when I was able to risk asking for their prayers) taught me humility in sharing burdens and the simple joy of trusting others.

"In God I trust. I will not be afraid," wrote the psalmist. These are powerful words of *encouragement*. Powerful words of *promise*. Powerful words of hope.

Powerful words!

Reflection Starters Twenty-One

Look at the service of Holy baptism (in both *The Book of Common Prayer* and *The Book of Alternative Services*) and reflect on the baptismal prayers.

> O Merciful God, grant that all sinful desires may die in *this Child* and that all things belonging to the Spirit may live and grow in *him*. Amen. Grant that *he* may have power and strength to have victory and to triumph against the devil, the world and the flesh. Amen. Grant that whosoever here shall begin to be of thy flock may evermore continue in the same. Amen. Grant that whosoever is here dedicated to thee by our office and ministry may also be endued with heavenly virtues and everlastingly rewarded through thy mercy, O blessed Lord God, who dost live and govern all things, world without end. Amen. (*BCP*, page 527)

> Heavenly Father, we thank you that by water and the Holy Spirit you have bestowed upon *these* your *servants* the forgiveness of sin, and have raised *them* to the new life of grace. Sustain *them*, O Lord, in your Holy Spirit. Give *them* an inquiring and discerning heart, the courage to will and to persevere, a spirit to know and to love you, and the gift of joy and wonder in all your works. Amen. (*BAS*, page 160)

How has the baptismal prayer said at your baptism come to fruition in your life and spiritual journey? Reflect on that in your Prayer Journal.

Have you ever been aware of the prayers of others interceding on your behalf?

In your Prayer Journal, reflect on how knowing that others were praying for you made you feel, and what you learned or discovered.

If you've not asked others to pray for you, what do you think might have restricted or limited or stopped you? Reflect on this in your Prayer Journal.

What would be necessary for you to trust God through the prayer ministry of others? Consider this in your Prayer Journal.

Chapter Twenty-Two

The twenty-third psalm that begins, "The Lord is my shepherd," continues to be a very special one in my life. My soul was being restored, as was that of my son. Each day brought new spiritual growth, new awareness, new insights, new surprises — and disturbances!

One day, my son expressed interest in returning to school — not high school but college. As I had been tutoring him at home, I thought that he could easily get his high school equivalency. But to write those tests, he had to be at least nineteen years of age. He was barely fifteen.

His old self-assurance was emerging when he said, "I'm going to get a calendar of classes and make an appointment with someone at the college, to see if I can enter school this fall."

He applied to the local college, and having passed the scrutiny of the panel that decided which students could enter under special student status, he was admitted. In time, he graduated with an Associate in Arts degree (with a major in media communications) and began his own company, VisionMedia Communications.

Miracle — pure and simple! There simply is no other way to account for his return to his former happy, self-assured self.

Reflection Starters Twenty-Two

Read the twenty-third psalm in various translations of the Bible.

When you have found a version you especially like, take each phrase individually, and reflect on the significance of the psalm in your life and spiritual journey. For example,

- "The Lord is my Shepherd." How is the Lord your shepherd?
- "I shall not want." How is it that you shall not want?

Record your thoughts in your Prayer Journal.

Chapter Twenty-Three

As I grow in my awareness and understanding of God, I remember earlier unrecognized instances of God's presence in my life — times when my world seemed bleak, dark, and lonely. Yet it was at just those moments when God had carried me and sustained me. One such instance revolved around my son's birth.

Due to a severe case of endometriosis in my early twenties, I was told that I would probably never conceive a child. If I did conceive, I wouldn't be able to carry the child to full term.

When my son was born, something within me wanted him always to remember that he was a gift from God. So to rhyme with God, this child was named Todd — a popular boy's name at the time. For years he was known as Todd (with two d's).

One day, when he asked me to tell him one of his favorite stories (the story of his birth), he said, "Mom, how many d's does God's name have?"

"Now what was going on in his head?" I wondered. "You know the answer to that question. What are you thinking of?" I asked.

"Well," he thoughtfully replied, "You told me that I was given the name Todd to remind me that I was a gift from

God. But God's name has only one d. Can I change my name to Tod, with one d?"

Reflecting on my pregnancy, the lengthy delivery, his illnesses over the years (celiac disease, hyperactivity, severe allergic response to UFFI, kidney problems), his various hospitalizations, and his emotional reactions to the marital difficulties and food allergies, I realized that God had been directing me long ago.

I just didn't know
at the time
that it was God's voice
directing me to name my son, Tod.

I just didn't know
at the time
that it was God's hand
protecting my son
through many troubles.

I just didn't know
at the time!

But, was it important to know at the time? Or was it simply sufficient to trust God?

Reflection Starters Twenty-Three

Have there been times when you "just didn't know" God was protecting; directing; loving; guiding you or your loved ones? Reflect on some of those instances in your Prayer Journal.

Is there a story behind the name by which you are known? For example, were you named

- after a particular person? (a relative or family friend)
- for a particular month? (April, May, and so on)
- in celebration of a particular attribute? (Joy, Grace, Hope)
- in remembrance of a holiday season? (Carol, Chris, Holly)
- in keeping with alphabetical naming of children? (Kenneth, Kari, Kurt, Katherine, Kirk, Kyla)
- in acknowledgment of a celebrity? (Elvis)
- in recognition of individuality, for example, a spice or piece of furniture? (Sage, Tiffany)
- as a witness to biblical heritage? (Aaron, Deborah, Moses, James, Elijah, Elizabeth, John, Hannah, Paul, Judith, Samuel)
- in solidarity with cultural heritage? (Moe, Indira, Juan, Bayani, Marie, Raven, Sasha, Gustav, Helmut, Marta, Chitra)

Did you choose your own name? If so, what is its significance?

If you don't know your "naming story," spend some time researching it with family members.

In your Prayer Journal, reflect on the significance of the name(s) you were given at birth.

If you were named for a family member or friend of the family, try to learn something about him or her.

- You might want to connect in person or communicate in writing if she or he is still alive.
- You might offer a prayer of thanksgiving for them.

In so doing, you may discover a part of yourself that had not been realized, discovered, or "celebrated."

Chapter Twenty-Four

Trust God! But trust, even in the "disturbances" of my life?

Yes! Each disturbance has deepened my walk with Christ. Each has drawn me into a closer relationship with the One who called me to recognize that I had been given gifts which I was to accept and use to God's glory in ways God directed.

After serving my curacy, I again sought God's direction. My bishop suggested that I let my name stand for the vacant position of a two-point parish in a rural coastal community.

In the country? But I was a city person. Whatever would I do in such a location? And two churches? They needed someone with years of parochial experience, not a new ordinand.

Challenged by my bishop's confidence in me, I decided to consider the possibility of moving to this parish and shared its self-description with my son. Tod's response was clear. "I think you should at least consider the parish. You've got tomorrow off, and I have no classes. How about we drive there and have a look?"

We did. On the ride home, we were both silent. Finally, Tod said, "Mom, I think God can really use your gifts there." So began the next part of God's disturbance in my life. The five years I spent in that parish taught me much!

By the grace of God, the two-point parish grew — spiritually, numerically, financially. We were able to hire a curate and eventually separate the two churches into two parishes. Ministry was rich and fulfilling. I loved the ocean and slow-paced living of the parish. I was beginning to think that I might even stay long enough to pay off the mortgage on my home.

But shortly after the separation of the two churches, I received a phone call inviting me to consider applying for a vacant parish in the city.

In the city? I'd grown to love rural ministry. Put me back into the city with the noise, the pollution, the crowding, the high cost of houses, the lack of parking? No thanks.

Several months later, my archdeacon phoned again to ask why I hadn't made an application. I had no reasonable answer. The parish was at a turning point in its history. This was an opportune time to leave.

I heard him say, "Don't you think God can speak through others — even me, your archdeacon?" If I were to be obedient to discerning God's plan for my life, I had to consider the parish.

I could not imagine myself in a city parish, but as I sought God's direction, I sensed that I should at least submit the application. Much to my surprise, I was invited to become the parish's next incumbent.

Ministry in the city was challenging, and God continued to disturb my life!

Reflection Starters Twenty-Four

Reflect on the gifts God has given you.

How have you used those gifts?

Has it been to God's glory or to your own personal edification? Reflect on this in your Prayer Journal.

Have you ever experienced God speaking to you through others? Reflect on one such instance in your Prayer Journal.

Chapter Twenty-Five

Another disturbance from God occurred when a colleague from a different diocese was visiting and shared a rumour she'd heard. It seemed that I was being considered as a possible candidate for diocesan bishop.

I did not react outwardly when she spoke. But inside, I was stressed. I found myself wondering where the difficulty came from. I slowly discovered that it had a lot to do with the call to ministry, and the depth to which I would really be willing to serve God. The idea of women in the episcopacy was certainly not yet universally accepted. Did I really want to break new ground in this way?

To that point in my ministry, I thought I'd been willing to serve God where I believed God had called me — suburban ministry, rural ministry, urban ministry, and ministry of administration on committees at various levels of the church. But would I be willing to serve in the North? In the East? As a bishop?

I heard myself say, "God, surely you wouldn't call me to any of those," but I wondered what my reaction would be if, one day, God did extend such an invitation. Would I even be willing to consider the possibility?

A quick response to such possibilities was, "No, because the North is too cold, the East is too busy, the episcopacy is too . . ." Through all this pondering, I felt God gently inviting me to give consideration to my responses and to prayerfully reconsider my whole attitude of call.

I remembered the words of a priest, years ago. When he discovered that I was reluctant to actively pursue ordination, primarily because I didn't like the idea, he said, "You're not called to like what God sets before you. You're called to faithfully and obediently respond."

Faithfully and obediently respond. Had I prayed about the possibility? Had I asked God? No, I had not, because I was sure I knew what God's response would be — "Open the door to the possibility." I chose not to open any such door. My prayer life was becoming distracted.

Now that an invitation had been formally extended, I told the parish wardens and asked for their prayers. Their encouragement that I consider the possibility of allowing my name to stand was affirming.

When, at last, I said to God that I was "willing to be willing" to serve as bishop if that were God's will, I received a strong indication that it was not. I awoke at three o'clock in the morning, and was aware of God speaking to my spirit, saying, "I have other plans for you at this time."

Immediately I went back to sleep and, for the first time since the whole issue confronted me, slept deeply and soundly. The next morning, I awoke with an incredible sense of peace. I wrote the Search and Nominations Committee and declined the nomination.

Little did I know that I would soon be called to ministry in a new way — beyond my diocese, beyond my country. The next step in my spiritual journey, God's next disturbance in my life, took me halfway around the world, to Sri Lanka, formerly known as Ceylon.

Reflection Starters Twenty-Five

In what ways has God called you to serve? Reflect on this in your Prayer Journal.

Have you always been obedient in responding to that call? If you have not, consider what prohibited you from doing so. Reflect on this in your Prayer Journal.

Are there any ways you are not, or have not been, willing to be willing to serve God? For example,

- particular vocation,
- forgiving yourself,
- using your gifts,
- forgiving another.

Reflect on those ways in your Prayer Journal.

Have you ever experienced an aspect of your personhood (gender, physical disability, mental handicap, emotional distress, race, language, age, and so on) to be a block for others? If so, spend time reflecting on those situations.

Using your Prayer Journal, record some of those times. Allow your feelings to surface.

- Remember the feelings when the situation occurred.
- Invite the Holy Spirit to help you deal with those feelings.
- Reflect on your present-day feelings as you remember the situation.

Peace

The peace of God,
which passes all understanding,
will guard your heart and mind in Christ Jesus
— Philippians 4:7

Chapter Twenty-Six

While participating at a World Council of Churches Consortium on Ecumenical Leadership Formation in Geneva, I met a priest from Sri Lanka who expressed his hope that someday I would go to his country, so that people there might experience the ministry of an ordained woman.

After he had been ordained bishop, the invitation came through formal channels. "When could I go?", came the question from overseas. It seemed that God's plan included a trip to Sri Lanka.

Another event confirmed the correctness of my accepting this ministry opportunity. The bishop of our partner diocese (of Northern Argentina) was visiting to tell us about his diocese. After linking his experience as a missionary with what I was about to do in Sri Lanka, the bishop invited those present to gather around, lay hands on me, and pray for my protection and ministry there.

I was deeply touched by the prayers of God's people and profoundly aware of God affirming my call to Sri Lanka at that time.

Further evidence came the Sunday before I was to leave for Sri Lanka. At the conclusion of the early Sunday morning service, one of the church wardens ushered me to the front of the church and then invited worshippers to "send me forth" with God's blessing.

Prayer, again, surrounding and encouraging me.

That same morning, during the main Sunday service, I spent time with the children (who had expressed fears for my safety), reassuring them that the God who loved them and watched over them in Canada, was the same God who loved me and would watch over me in Sri Lanka. Before the children left the sanctuary for their Sunday school time, I found myself surrounded by them and their teachers who gently laid hands on me and prayed. At the end of the service, other parishioners gathered around to pray.

I was in awe of God's powerful presence and profoundly aware of that precious peace "that passes all understanding." Surrounded by prayer, I was ready for whatever lay ahead.

The next day, as I said good-bye to my mother, son, and friend from the parish who had driven me to the airport, I was given an envelope with instructions that it be opened on the airplane. As the plane lifted off the tarmac, I remembered the envelope and opened it to find a card with a schedule of parishioners who would keep a daily prayer vigil for my ministry while I was away.

Tears flooded my eyes, as I realized God's hand in the whole trip, beginning five years earlier in Geneva, Switzerland!

Reflection Starters Twenty-Six

Have you ever experienced the laying on of hands

- for healing?
- for protection?
- for blessing?

Reflect on those incidents in your Prayer Journal and recall how you experienced God's presence in each instance.

Consider your spiritual life five years ago. Prayerfully reflect on the time from then to the present time in your life.

In your Prayer Journal, reflect on the occasions in the past five years when God guided your decisions.

Have you ever been aware of the "peace that passes all understanding"? Reflect on one or two of those instances in your Prayer Journal.

Chapter Twenty-Seven

The invitation to go to Sri Lanka as the first woman priest to "visit and break bread among us" was a great privilege. In the words of the Bishop of Colombo, I was to be a "visual teaching aid," a "sacramental sign" among the people who had never experienced the ministry of a woman priest.

While others had different expectations for my visit, I knew deep within my spirit that I was there to provide a "ministry of presence," to simply "be" — be myself — and let God touch people's hearts and open people's minds to the possibility of the ordination of women in Sri Lanka.

For much of my visit, I stayed in the bishop's residence, which was situated on the cathedral grounds. As a result, I was able to begin several days with a spiritually nourishing celebration of the holy eucharist in the early morning tranquillity.

Many in Canada were praying for God's will to be done through my ministry in Sri Lanka. During the prayers of the people at those morning eucharists, I discovered that the same intention figured in the daily prayers of many in Sri Lanka as well.

It was a powerful expression of partnership — a partnership of prayer.

As I faxed the people of the parish I served in Canada, I realized that the prayer connection which bound Sri Lankans and Canadians together in the Spirit sustained me when feelings of isolation and "being different" flooded my thoughts, and when I asked God for answers to my jumbled questions about the poverty and injustices in the country around me.

Reflection Starters Twenty-Seven

What is your understanding of a "ministry of presence"? Are you aware of God ever using you in such a ministry?

When have you been used in such a way? Reflect on a recent occasion in your Prayer Journal.

Have you ever experienced a "partnership of prayer" (a prayer connection), a time when you were praying for someone and knew they were praying for you?

How would you describe that partnership of prayer experience? Spend some time reflecting on one such instance in your Prayer Journal.

Chapter Twenty-Eight

In many instances, after being exposed to the ministry of a woman priest, those who initially stated that they were against the ordination of women in Sri Lanka discovered that they were open to the possibility. Some even completely changed their attitude.

One response from a person known for his opposing views on the subject demonstrated the way people can change. He said, "In the eucharist, I experienced being fed and nourished by my mother. And it was good!"

At gatherings arranged by the bishops, there was representation by both those who seemed open and those who seemed opposed to the ordination of women. I had been advised that there would likely be strong and vocal opposition, but thanks be to God, I experienced open discussion, genuine concern, and sincerity in seeking God's will.

I was aware of God working gently, quietly, to blow away cobwebs of doubt, fear, and threat. It was a time of watching God transform opinions and open hearts and minds to the possibilities of new ways of partnership in ministry.

It was also a time of personal learning. I soon came to realize that cognitive awareness resulting from reading, watching videos, television, or movies is no substitute for experiential reality. For instance —

I knew Sri Lanka was experiencing political conflict in the east and north, but I didn't anticipate my reaction to the solemn-faced security guards at the roadblocks in the capital city of Colombo and peaceful rural areas. This is a country at war, and the silent sentries with loaded guns never let you forget it!

I knew there would be breathtakingly magnificent scenery, but I didn't anticipate the dirt and garbage along the roadsides which polluted the air, infiltrated the curbside food stalls, permeated everything I ate, touched, read, breathed, and wore.

I knew there would be wonderful fragrances of tropical flowers and exotic fruit, but I didn't anticipate the smells of rotting garbage heaped by the roadside, or the diesel fumes belching from the vans, buses, and cars that clogged the roads.

I knew there would be poverty the likes of which I'd never before experienced, but I didn't anticipate seeing mothers wash naked babies in dirty ditch water on a main street in the capital city of the country, or seeing malnourished newborns amid the squalid and cramped conditions of refugee centres.

Yet, in the midst of terrible conditions there were, incredibly, signs of hope!

In a very small room at the back of a refugee center, four women taught songs to pre-school children. Since there was no room to sit, they all stood for this brief respite from the noisy, hot, humid, dusty, and impossibly crowded communal living area.

The children seemed oblivious to their situation and greeted me with smiles and giggles when I knelt down to be at their level and tried to speak their language.

On the door, crudely printed, were these words, "Life is a gift from God." In their desperate situation, there was still hope!

I was reminded of a similar saying on one of the walls in Dachau:

I believe in the sun, even when it is not shining.
I believe in the stars, even when I see them not.
I believe in God, even when God is silent.

In the midst of a terrifying yesterday, a bleak and often hungry today, a potentially fearful tomorrow (for they never know if they will be taken in for questioning), there is hope!

Reflection Starters Twenty-Eight

Have you ever served on a church committee, council, board, or synod (in a parish, diocese, ecclesiastical province, or at the national level)?

In your Prayer Journal, reflect on the decision-making process of those bodies. For example,

- the steps leading up to the decision,
- how the decisions were made (i.e. consensus, majority),
- some consequences resulting from decisions made.

Are you aware of any differences between the above process and that followed by secular organizations you've served (volunteer, place of employment)?

Consider moments in your life when you were aware of God "opening hearts and minds," moments when opinions were transformed because of God's grace working in and through the process and people. Reflect on those moments in your Prayer Journal.

Pretend that you are a student in a high school English class. Your teacher has just given you the title of a writing assignment, "Life is a Gift from God." In your Prayer Journal, write an essay on that title, letting your pen flow, not editing as you write.

When you've completed your essay, sit quietly and offer it to the One who gave you the gift of life.

Chapter Twenty-Nine

At a meeting with about a hundred women, an unpremeditated plan surfaced to strategize for the ordination of women in Sri Lanka.

One woman in the group asked me to give a name to their movement. I responded that the name needed to come from among themselves. I sensed though, that the word *movement* probably shouldn't be included, because it often suggests negative connotations and evokes unsupportive responses.

As I went to sleep that evening, my prayer included something like,

Dear God, please continue to encourage the men and women of this country around the issue of women's ordination; and give them a name by which they can begin to gather support. Amen.

That night, I had a dream. Big flakes of snow drifted gently over a wide expanse of country. Then I saw the initials SNOW.

When I awoke, I looked at my little notebook by my bed and found those same initials. Thinking that the extreme heat of Sri Lanka (90 plus each day!) was the cause of such a dream, I paid little attention to it. But in my morning devotions, God seemed to be inviting me to reconsider the dream. So I did, asking the Holy Spirit to reveal the dream's meaning.

Again, the letters SNOW appeared. But this time, rather

than standing *beside* each other, they stood *under* each other. Curious about the interpretation, I asked God to show me what the letters meant and, ever so plainly, came the response —

Support
Network for the
Ordination of
Women

Wow! When God speaks, it is awesome!

At breakfast the next morning, after sharing my dream with the bishop's wife, she noted that it would probably "soon be SNOWing in Sri Lanka."

As the plane left the tarmac in the early hours of the morning, I was overwhelmed by what I had learned, witnessed, and experienced during my visit. Overwhelmed with a sense of pain and sadness for the Sri Lankans who continue to live in the midst of civil conflict. Overwhelmed with feelings of awe at God's timing, creative responses, and encouragement of the possibility of the ordination of women.

God had disturbed my life again, this time in a land far from home. What next?

Reflection Starters Twenty-Nine

Have you ever experienced God speaking to you in a dream? In your Prayer Journal, recall one such dream and reflect on its possible significance in your spiritual journey.

If you've not experienced God in this way, consider consciously preparing yourself to "hear" God while you're asleep. For example,

- Put a notepad beside your bed before retiring for the night.
- Before going to sleep, offer a prayer, inviting God to communicate with you while you sleep. For example,

Re-creating God,

As my body rests this night, I pray that my spirit is open to receive your word.

When I waken in the morning, help me to interpret the meaning of the words and symbols I put on my paper beside my bed during the night.

I recommit myself to you this night — body, mind and spirit. This I ask in the name of your Son who taught his disciples to pray . . .

(Close with the Lord's Prayer.) Amen.

When the next "disturbance" in your spiritual journey comes, how will you greet it? You might want to offer a prayer to God, in your Prayer Journal, about how you would like to respond.

Afterword

How and where will the next disturbance occur? I don't know. But I do know that there will be disturbances, because on this faith journey I still have much to learn about God, ministry, the Anglican Communion, and about myself.

God does disturb lives — challenging, confronting, inviting us to "taste and see" more of the implications of living a Christ-centered life, of faithfully fulfilling our baptismal ministry.

As we allow God to disturb us, as we risk opening another door along our spiritual journey, as we make ourselves vulnerable, we say Yes to God.

Yes, God
I'm willing to be open . . .
to exploring possibilities,
to learning a new lesson,
to experiencing a new birth.

Even if I
endure a suffering.

Even if I
struggle through a dry valley period.

Even if I
bring closure to a part of my life.

As we allow God to disturb our lives,
we are drawn more deeply
into relationship with the One

who bled
for us

who died
for us

who rose
for us

who lives
with us

Thanks be to God!

Epilogue

For as long as I can recall
this journey of faithfulness
to the One who calls
has been like
a circular staircase
around
down
around
up
around.

Just when I think that
a lesson is learned
a valley survived
a birth delivered
an experience lived
a suffering endured
a mountain climbed
an ending completed

new
lessons, valleys
births
experiences, sufferings
mountains
endings
surface

and I learn
once more
what it is

to hope
to rejoice
to trust
to accept
to love
to forgive
to give thanks

for
the One who calls

for
all that has

for
all who have brought me

to
through
beyond

Only
to re-learn
to re-do
to re-experience
it all again

differently!

My life is content. Why disturb it?

but

it *is*
disturbed

it *has been*
disturbed

it *will continue*
to be disturbed

I am called
it seems

to serve
a disturbing God.

Thanks be to God!

Methods for Reflection

Disturbed by God invites people to reflect and pray as they make connections between the author's personal story and their own faith story. The following suggestions might help readers work with the material and their own faith experiences.

Individual Reflection: Prayer Journal

A Prayer Journal is a personal notebook where one might record thoughts about, reactions to, or remembrances of particular moments in life — moments when God interacted with one's spiritual journey. Recording dreams, daily activities, and insights during the day are often helpful in uncovering and recognizing the many times God has touched or "disturbed" one's daily activities, experiences, and decisions. Keeping a Prayer Journal can be a wondrous opening for the Holy Spirit to enter lives and encourage people to a deeper understanding and discovery of who they are, who God is for them, and how God speaks today.

How to begin? Make your own Prayer Journal. One inexpensive way is to write on loose-leaf paper and insert pages into a binder. Other ways might include purchasing a fabric covered notebook or recording in a computer. Some practical suggestions —

- After dating each entry, allow the words to flow onto the paper. Don't pre-judge the validity of any entry.

- Periodically, take time to reread your entries, and record your reactions to these new entries (allowing the Holy Spirit to encourage you in this inner dialogue).

The method of journalling isn't important. Just begin, and anticipate a deepening of your spiritual awareness — discovering God in the midst of pain, joy, suffering, loneliness, fear, anxiety, questioning, and celebration. Your Prayer Journal can be a continuing record of "disturbances" from God.

As journal writings are personal conversations with oneself and God, they generally are not meant to be shared with others. However, you may find it helpful to share parts of your Prayer Journal with a soul friend or spiritual director. Some of the Reflection Starters might raise additional faith questions, in which case it might be helpful to seek the guidance of another. (Glossary of Terms: *Soul Friend, Spiritual Director,* p.127).

For further reading —

Broyles, Ann. *Journaling: A Spirit Journey.* Nashville: The Upper Room, 1988.

Fenhagen, James. *More than Wanderers: Spiritual Disciplines for Christian Ministry.* San Francisco: Harper and Row, 1978.

Group Reflection: Group Study

This method relies on the reader's connection with at least one other person who is, at the same time, reading *Disturbed by God.* This connection can be casual. That is, two or three friends who get together for coffee on a regular basis might share their insights about reading the book. Study and reflection of this book thus provides a good reason to get together, to know one another better, and to deepen the spiritual walk in an unstructured way.

The connection can be intentional. For example,

- A group of clergy could use *Disturbed by God* as an opportunity to share their views on various aspects of the Christian journey.

- Cursillistas (people who have attended a Cursillo weekend) might use the book as a focus for the study component of their Fourth Day group.

- A parish or deanery study group could use the book as an Advent, Lenten, Easter, or Summer study book.

- A husband and wife could use the book as a tool to help them communicate with one another on a regular basis about their respective spiritual journeys.

Participants in any study group might individually read several chapters ahead of time, perhaps recording their responses to the Reflection Starters in their Prayer Journal. At each group session, participants might discuss which questions from *Disturbed by God* challenged them, which ones surprised them, which ones helped them make connections with their own "story," and how that came to be.

A leader isn't necessary, but a facilitator would be an asset. To facilitate open and flowing discussion among participants, the facilitator might

- Remind participants of the importance of confidentiality (nothing that is shared within the group discussion is to be shared beyond the group);

- Respect an individual's right to non self-disclosure

(share only that which she or he is comfortable sharing);

- Prepare for each session by praying for participants;
- Enable conversation to flow by inviting all to participate, yet reminding them to do so at their own comfort level. (The Anglican *via-media* (middle road) may be a good rule of thumb here — "All may, some will, none should").
- Invite participants to sing James Manley's song, "Spirit, Spirit of Gentleness" (reproduced below) and share thoughts with one another about the images of a disturbing God and a spirit of restlessness.

Spirit, Spirit of Gentleness

Refrain
Spirit, spirit of gentleness, blow thro' the wilderness calling and free.
Spirit, spirit of restlessness, stir me from placidness, Wind, Wind on the sea.

You moved on the waters, you called to the deep, then you coaxed up the mountains from the valleys of sleep; and over the aeons you called to each thing; wake from your slumbers and rise on your wings.

You swept thro' the desert, you stung with the sand and you goaded your people with a law and a land; and when they were blinded with their idols and lies then you spoke thro' your prophets to open their eyes.

You sang in a stable, you cried from a hill, then you whispered in silence when the whole world was still;

and down in the city you called once again
when you blew thro' your people, on the rush of the
   wind.

You call from tomorrow, you break ancient schemes,
from the bondage of sorrow the captives dream dreams;
our women see visions, our men clear their eyes,
with bold new decisions, your people arise.

- Delegate roles (if appropriate) of "prayer-opener," "prayer-closer," and "refreshment-arranger" (refreshments can be a good way of building community).

Some suggestions for the "prayer-opener" person —

1. At the beginning of each session, the lighting of a candle might help participants disengage from the busyness of their day.
   - Encourage participants to relax and prayerfully enter into the study
   - Give participants an opportunity to be still and let God speak to them in the silence, discussions, and personal reflections.

2. Perhaps, after a moment of silence (just before the discussion begins), saying (or singing) a prayer in unison (see below for a suggestion) might help participants feel connected with one another.
   - Focus their attention on hearing God's voice in the group discussions and personal reflections.

Be with us, O God, on our journey this day.
Help us discuss, reflect, journal, we pray.
Keep us alert and help us discern
What is your will as together we learn."

(Can be sung to "Be Thou My Vision," Slane 10 10 10 10.)

Some suggestions for the "prayer-closer" person —

1. Closure time can include a time of silence for individual journal writing where participants might record their thoughts, insights, questions gleaned from the discussion.

2. The session could conclude with silent or corporate prayer and perhaps end with the "grace," "The grace of our Lord, Jesus Christ, and the love of God, and the fellowship of the Holy Spirit be with us all. Amen."

Approaches to Prayer

There are probably as many approaches to prayer as there are individuals who pray, as this anonymous poem indicates.

I know not by what methods rare,
But this I know: God answers prayer.
I know that God has given the Word
Which tells me prayer is always heard
And will be answered, soon or late.
And so I pray and calmly wait.

I know not if the blessing sought
Will come in just the way I thought,
But leave my prayers with God alone
Whose will is wiser than my own,
Assured that God will grant my quest,
Or send some answer far more blest.

God always answers prayer in some way! The words of the prophet Jeremiah are a wonderful beginning point for prayer.

"For I know the plans I have for you," says the Lord. "They are plans for good and not for evil; to give you a future and a hope. In those days when you pray, I will listen. You will find me when you seek me; if you look for me with all your heart" (Jeremiah 29:11–13).

Prayer is a way of communicating with God — talking with God (sharing joys, sorrows, concerns, anger), and listening to God (for comforting reassurance, for sense of hope).

Prayer helps maintain an open and intimate relationship with the One who called us into being, and sustains and nurtures us along our spiritual journey.

Quite simply, prayer can be described as the activity of opening your heart to God and expectantly waiting for God's renewing power within your life. To faithfully live out one's baptismal ministry, a personal daily life of prayer is integral.

Along my faith journey, I came across the Ten R's of Prayer, but I don't know who wrote them. I share them in the hope that they will prove as helpful to readers as they have been to me, and pray that reprinting them here is not in violation of copyright.

The Ten R's of Prayer

Relax. You can't pray if you're tense, conscious of the clock. Deep breathing may help you relax and "turn off" from the stresses of your life.

Realize God's presence with you, in and through the silence.

Release your deepest feelings, your most pressing concerns in God's presence, the Holy One, who called you into being and loves you, unconditionally.

Reflect on your daily experiences of love, fear, need, sorrow, joy, anger — giving God the time and opportunity to give you the grace to see God in all things, situations, and people.

Repent of your sins and ask God's forgiveness.

Renew your trust in the One who has sustained you, as you remember how God has led you in the past, and accept God's forgiveness of your sins.

Read a passage from Scripture each day, slowly and meditatively considering "What is God saying to me through these words in my situations of today?"

Relate. Think through the day ahead with a renewed sensitivity to God's presence and call. Ask God to help you to raise your thoughts, your words, your behaviour, to what God would have you do, say, and think.

Remember people in need, one by one — family, friends, people you dislike — letting God bring peace, love and healing through your prayers. Remember yourself — a much loved, specifically chosen child of God, called into being with a purpose in this world.

Rededicate your life afresh to God and move back into the world with peace in your heart, willing and eager to serve Christ.

For further reading —

Green, Thomas. *Opening to God: A Guide to Prayer.* Notre Dame: Ave Maria Press, 1977.

Leech, Kenneth. *True Prayer: An Introduction to Christian Spirituality.* London: Sheldon Press, 1877.

Metropolitan Anthony. *Living Prayer.* London: Darton, Longman & Todd, London, 1966.

Prater, Arnold. *Prayer Partners: Spiritual Enrichment for Your Marriage.* Nashville: Abingdon Press, 1987.

Glossary of Terms

Some recommended reading for each glossary term follows each entry.

Baptism (see also *Baptismal Ministry*)

Baptism is a sign of new life in Christ. It is a public proclamation of saying Yes to Christ. It is a time when a person is "born again" into a new union with Jesus Christ and publicly declares him- or herself to be a Christian. Baptism, happening only once in a life, is a turning point. The rite of baptism is celebrated within the life of a worshipping community, usually at the time of the primary Sunday morning service of worship. As one receives the water of baptism (either by immersion or by sprinkling), one "lets go and lets God" enter life in a new and creative way.

For further reading —

Ingham, Michael. *Rites for a New Age: Understanding the Book of Alternative Services.* Toronto: Anglican Book Centre, 1986 (especially pages 137–162).

Ross, Robert. *Preparing for Baptism Using the Book of Alternative Services.* Toronto: Anglican Book Centre, 1993.

Stuchbery, Ian. *This is Our Faith: A Guide to the Life and Belief for Anglicans with a Revised Chapter in Worship.* Toronto: Anglican Book Centre, 1990.

Baptismal Ministry (see also *Baptism*)

Based on the practice of the early church (which developed the practice of baptism), becoming a Christian "has much to do with learning to live the new lifestyle within the Christian community as it [does] with specific beliefs" (*The Book of Alternative Services*, page 146).

The baptismal covenant is a call to ministry in the world — daily to "proclaim by word and example, the good news of God in Christ; seek and serve Christ in all persons, loving neighbour as self; strive for justice and peace among all people; respect the dignity of every human being" (*The Book of Alternative Services*, page 159).

How one exercises one's baptismal ministry (which can be expressed as lay person, priest, deacon, bishop), is largely dependent on the identification and use of gifts given by God. The apostle Paul wrote that "our gifts differ according to the grace given us." Scripture offers three major references to spiritual gifts (Ephesians 4, 1 Corinthians 12, Romans 12), with passing references to gifts throughout both the Old and New Testaments of the Bible. Each person is given at least one gift and is called to use that gift in service to others.

Confirmation

In the Anglican Church of Canada, the rite of Confirmation is simply the confirming of one's baptismal promises.

Confirmation involves the public renewal of commitment to Christ, the declaration of membership in the Anglican Communion, and the "sending forth" in the power of the Holy Spirit "to perform the service set before them." Thus, through Confirmation, one recommits oneself to baptismal ministry in the world. (See also *Baptism* and *Baptismal Ministry*.)

For further reading —

Holmes, Urban. *What is Anglicanism?* Toronto: Anglican Book Centre, 1982.

Stott, John. *Your Confirmation,* London: Hodden & Stoughton, 1958.

Wilkinson, Raymond. *An Adult Confirmation Candidate's Handbook.* London: Faith Press, 1964.

Laying on of Hands

Practiced by the earliest Christians as they prayed over the sick (James 5:14), the laying on of hands is a rite of healing touch. *The Book of Alternative Services* notes that by the laying on of hands, "they made known the healing power and presence of God" (page 555).

For further reading —

Thomas, Leo & Alkire, Jan. *Healing as a Parish Ministry: Mending Body, Mind and Spirit.* Notre Dame: Ave Maria Press, 1992.

Ordination

Three distinct orders of ordained ministry have been characteristic of the church since the time of the New Testament.

As *The Book of Alternative Services* notes, the order of bishops carries on "the apostolic work of leading, supervising, and uniting the Church"; the presbyters or priests "together with the bishops" share "in the governance of the Church, in the carrying out of its missionary and pastoral work, and in the preaching of the word of God and the administration of God's holy sacraments"; the deacons, "in addition to assisting bishops and priests in the above, have a special responsibility to minister in Christ's name to the poor, the sick, the suffering, and the helpless" (page 631).

For further reading —

Neill, Stephen. *Anglicanism*. Middlesex, England: Penguin Books, 1958.

Prayer Journal

See section on *Methods for Reflection* (p. 115).

Soul Friend: Spiritual Director

In every decision in life, there are many factors to consider. For the Christian, there is a basic question to be asked: "What does God want me to do in this situation?"

For many, exploration about where one is going in their relationship with God, how their prayer life is developing, and where God is at work in their daily life is often ignored. A soul friend or spiritual director is someone who can suggest questions to think and pray about, so that spiritual growth can continue in an intentional manner. Such a person can be either ordained (deacon, priest, bishop) or a lay person particularly gifted in the area of listening, prayer, and spiritual guidance.

Where to begin? How about speaking with your priest or a lay person you consider particularly spiritually intuitive, or reading something on the subject?

For further reading —

Barry, William & Connolly, W. *The Practice of Spiritual Direction*. New York: Seabury Press, 1982.

Edwards, Tilden. *Spiritual Friend*. New York: Paulist Press, 1980.

Jeff, George. *Spiritual Direction for Every Christian*. London: SPCK, 1987.

Leech, Kenneth *Soul Friend*. London: Sheldon Press, 1977.

Merton, Thomas. *Spiritual Direction*. London: SPCK, 1984.

Stairs, Jean. *Be My Companion: A Study of Spiritual Direction*. Toronto: Image Books, 1982